THE BOOK OF

REGIONAL AMERICAN COOKING

COWBOY

THE BOOK OF

REGIONAL AMERICAN COOKING

COWBOY

Stephen Glass

Photographed by
GLENN CORMIER

HPBooks

HPBooks
are published by The Berkley Publishing Group
200 Madison Avenue
New York, New York 10016

Special thanks for props to Crate and Barrel, San Diego; The Pottery Shack, Laguna Beach; Williams-Sonoma, San Diego; Qué Pasa, Scottsdale; and Yippee-ei-o, Phoenix.

Food stylist: Dave Pogul
Assistant food stylists: Jeffrey DeLeo and Alba Cera-Slavin

First edition: April 1995

Published simultaneously in Canada.

Library of Congress Cataloging-in-Publication Data

Glass, Stephen E.
   The book of regional American cooking. Cowboy / Stephen E. Glass
   — 1st ed.
         p.   cm.
   Includes index.
   ISBN 1-55788-197-9 (pbk. : alk. paper)
   1. Cookery, American—Western style.   I. Title.
TX715.2.W47G53 1995
641.5978—dc20   94-28040
                                                              CIP

PRINTED IN HONG KONG

10 9 8 7 6 5 4 3 2 1

This book is printed on acid-free paper.

Notice: The information printed in this book is true and complete to the best of our knowledge. All recommendations are made without any guarantees on the part of the author or the publisher. The author and publisher disclaim all liability in connection with the use of this information.

CONTENTS

Introduction 7

Cooking in a Dutch Oven 8

Appetizers 11

Soups 18

Breakfast 21

Meats 35

Poultry 53

Fish 61

Side Dishes 64

Breads 81

Desserts 94

Metric Charts 113

Index 115

INTRODUCTION

Cowboy or western cooking covers a broad range of foods because of the wide geographic area over which cattle ranching was spread as well as the evolution of the lifestyle associated with the industry itself. The real cowboy, the herder who spent from dawn to dusk in the saddle, generally had a very limited menu—black coffee, beans, and bacon, with variety being the sequence in which he ate the three.

Cattle growing and ranching extended from east Texas west to the Pacific Ocean, and from Mexico north to Idaho and Montana. Ranch cooking was diverse and varied greatly with the region; it was influenced by the ethnic background of the rancher and the region in which he lived. Most ranches had a garden that produced fruits and vegetables, as the local soil and climate would allow, and a variety of farm animals to supplement the primarily beef diet.

Each ethnic group that settled the West brought many of their favorite recipes with them and simply adjusted them to accommodate the ingredients available locally. Many western dishes are easily traced back to their Native American, Spanish, Basque, Chinese, or any number of other ethnic origins.

During the long cattle drives of the late 1800s a "chuck wagon," or an early kitchen on wheels, provided the drovers with meals of sustenance, variety, and oftentimes, ingenuity. The chuck wagon was stocked with dry goods, such as beans, flour, coffee, and cornmeal. Fresh vegetables were rare, and meat was obtained from the herds the cowboys were driving, supplemented with wild game taken along the way. One person, the cookie, was in charge of all meals as well as the medical requirements of the cowboys. His rules concerning the chuck wagon had to be strictly followed or he could become very temperamental.

The dude ranch, where city slickers can dress up and pretend to be cowboys or simply enjoy spending time on a ranch, became a popular getaway during the late 1940s. The dude ranches of today offer many of the amenities of other vacation resorts, including an appealing cuisine, with a western flair, of course.

The recipes in this book include samples of the many types of western cooking, from boiled coffee and Dutch Oven Biscuits, to Steak Ranchero and Migas. All the food will taste better eaten under a western sky, but all the dishes can be prepared in a home kitchen.

COOKING IN A DUTCH OVEN

A Dutch oven designed for cooking over charcoal or hot coals is made of heavy cast iron and has a lid with a lip to hold the briquettes and short legs that raise the bottom of the Dutch oven away from the briquettes. Cooking with charcoal is an easy way to standardize cooking times.

Always remember that a Dutch oven that has been preheated or is over hot charcoal is hot! Because the oven is made of heavy cast iron, it cools slowly and will stay hot enough to burn for several minutes after removal from the heat. Always use a heavy oven mitt.

First preheat the Dutch oven in a regular oven, over hot charcoal on a grill, or over campfire coals. Heat both the Dutch oven and its lid. Preheating ensures that the food will cook evenly and more quickly.

While the Dutch oven is heating, light charcoal briquettes for under the Dutch oven and for placing on the lid. Usually ten briquettes are under the oven and seven briquettes are placed on the lid. If the dish requires more than one hour of cooking time, more briquettes will have to be added to both the top and underside of the oven. Dishes that burn easily, such as some desserts, require less heat and fewer briquettes.

Place a piece of heavy-duty foil over a nonflammable surface such as sand or rocks. Evenly space the briquettes in a circle the size of the oven and place two briquettes in the center.

Place the Dutch oven with the food over the hot briquettes. Add the cover and place the briquettes evenly on the lid. To check for doneness, remove the lid with a heavy oven mitt and open the lid so the steam goes away from you. Be careful so ashes do not fall into the food.

All recipes that call for a traditional Dutch oven can also be cooked in a conventional oven. See the variation with each recipe.

USING A DUTCH OVEN

Place a piece of heavy-duty foil over a nonflammable surface such as sand or rocks (or perhaps a concrete or brick patio). Evenly space 8 hot charcoal briquettes on the foil in a circle the size of the oven and place 2 briquettes in the center, unless recipe calls for a smaller amount.

Place the preheated Dutch oven containing the food to be cooked directly over the hot briquettes. The legs of the Dutch oven will prevent the hot briquettes from touching the bottom of the oven.

Add the lid and place 10 (or number in recipe) hot briquettes evenly on the lid. To check for doneness, remove the lid with a heavy oven mitt—open the lid so the steam goes away from you. Be careful that ashes do not fall into the food. If food cooks longer than 1 hour, additional hot briquettes must be added to both lid and surface under Dutch oven unless recipe directs otherwise.

HOT HOT SALSA

2 medium-size jalapeño chiles
2 serrano chiles
6 medium-size tomatoes, diced
6 green onions with tops, finely
    chopped
1 cup water
1 medium-size onion, minced
1/2 cup finely chopped cilantro
1 tablespoon crushed hot chiles
1 teaspoon white wine vinegar
1 teaspoon salt

Wearing rubber gloves, mince jalapeño and
serrano chiles with a knife.

In a large bowl, combine all of the ingredients. Cover and refrigerate 1 hour before
serving.

Makes about 6 servings.

11

TORTILLA APPETIZER

1 (6-oz.) container soft cream cheese
1 fresh jalapeño chile, minced
4 (10-inch) flour tortillas

Combine cream cheese and chile in a small bowl.

Heat tortillas, one at a time, in a large ungreased skillet over low heat just until soft to prevent cracking while rolling.

With a small spatula, spread the chile-cream cheese mixture evenly over one side of each tortilla. Roll up each tortilla with the chile mixture on the inside, and cut into 1-inch pieces to serve.

Makes 6 to 8 servings.

Note
For neater slices, wrap tortillas in plastic wrap and refrigerate 30 minutes before slicing.

FRIED RATTLESNAKE

2 eggs
1 cup all-purpose flour
1/2 teaspoon garlic powder
Salt and freshly ground pepper
8 rattlesnake rounds (about 1/2 pound)
Vegetable oil for frying

Lightly beat eggs in a shallow bowl. Combine flour, garlic powder, salt, and pepper in another shallow bowl.

Rinse meat and pat dry; dip in egg and coat with flour mixture.

Add 2 inches of oil to a large skillet. Heat oil to 375F (190C) or until a 1-inch bread cube turns golden brown in 40 seconds. Drop meat into hot oil. Cook until golden brown. Drain on paper towels.

Makes 4 servings.

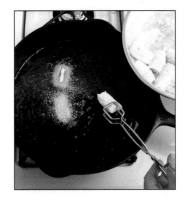

FRIED MOUNTAIN OYSTERS

6 mountain oysters
1/2 cup salt
1/2 cup distilled white vinegar
1 cup all-purpose flour
Salt and freshly ground pepper
Vegetable oil for frying

Soak mountain oysters 2 hours in a large bowl of water with salt and vinegar.

Remove mountain oysters from water and pat dry. Peel skin from oysters by making a slit lengthwise and cutting off the ends. Cut into 1-inch slices. Combine flour, salt, and pepper in a shallow bowl and coat slices with flour mixture.

Pour 2 inches of oil into a medium-size skillet. Heat oil to 365F (185C) or until a 1-inch bread cube turns golden brown in 60 seconds. Add mountain oysters in batches and fry until browned and crisp. Drain on paper towels.

Makes 4 servings.

Note
Mountain oysters are the testicles from young bulls. The cowboys would harvest them as part of the process of making bulls into steers during the roundup and cook them in the hot coals. They can be ordered from a specialty meat market.

SPICY BAKED WINGS

About 10 chicken wings
1/4 cup milk
1/2 cup dried bread crumbs
1/4 cup grated Parmesan cheese
1/2 teaspoon salt
1/2 teaspoon dried leaf thyme
1/4 teaspoon red (cayenne) pepper
Freshly ground black pepper

Garlic-Mustard Sauce:
1/4 cup mayonnaise
2 tablespoons buttermilk or plain
  yogurt
1 tablespoon Dijon mustard
2 garlic cloves, minced
2 tablespoons snipped chives

Preheat oven to 375F (190C). Grease a 13″ x 9″ baking pan. Cut wings into 3 pieces, cutting through joints. Reserve wing tips for making stock. Place remaining pieces in a medium-size bowl. Pour milk over chicken, turning to coat.

Combine crumbs, cheese, salt, thyme, cayenne, and black pepper in a shallow bowl. Dip chicken in crumb mixture to coat. Place in greased pan in a single layer. Bake about 30 minutes or until chicken is tender and crust is browned.

Prepare sauce: Combine all ingredients in a small bowl. Serve as a dipping sauce.

Makes about 20 appetizers.

BARBECUED WINGS

15 chicken wings

Barbecue Sauce:
1 tablespoon olive oil
1 medium-size onion, finely chopped
2 garlic cloves, minced
1-1/4 cups ketchup
1/4 cup packed brown sugar
2 tablespoons white vinegar
1 teaspoon Worcestershire sauce
1 teaspoon prepared mustard
1 jalapeño chile, minced

Preheat oven to 375F (190C). Grease a 13″ x 9″ baking pan. Place chicken in greased pan. Bake about 15 minutes.

Prepare sauce: Heat oil in a medium-size saucepan over medium heat. Add onion and garlic; cook until softened. Stir in ketchup, brown sugar, vinegar, Worcestershire sauce, mustard, and chile. Simmer 5 to 10 minutes.

Pour sauce over partially cooked wings. Bake 20 minutes or until chicken is tender and glazed.

Makes 15 appetizers.

SMOKED TROUT TRIANGLES

2 whole smoked trout or other
  smoked fish
1 (3-oz.) package light cream cheese,
  softened
2 tablespoons milk
1 teaspoon prepared horseradish
2 teaspoons Dijon mustard
2 tablespoons minced green onion tops
10 light rye bread slices, crusts removed
  and cut into squares or rectangles
1 bunch radishes, tops and roots
  removed and thinly sliced
Parsley leaves

Remove skin and bones from trout. Flake
trout into bite-size pieces.

Combine cream cheese, milk, horseradish,
mustard, and green onion in a medium-size
bowl. Beat until light and fluffy.

Spread cheese mixture on bread slices. Cut
each slice into 2 triangles. Arrange pieces of
trout, radishes, and parsley on cheese.

Makes 20 appetizers.

CORN CHOWDER

5 bacon slices, diced
1 medium-size onion, diced
1 cup boiling water
1 cup diced potatoes
1-1/2 cups cooked or canned
whole-kernel corn
1-1/2 cups whole milk
3 tablespoons butter or margarine
1/4 teaspoon salt
Coarsely ground pepper

Cook the bacon in a medium-size skillet over medium heat until partially cooked; add onion and cook until browned. Drain off most of fat. Add boiling water to onion and bacon mixture; simmer 3 or 4 minutes.

Put potatoes into a medium-size saucepan. Add bacon and onion mixture. Cook 5 minutes; add corn and cook until the potatoes are tender.

Add milk, butter, salt, and pepper. Heat just until hot; do not boil.

Makes 4 servings.

TURKEY SOUP

1 turkey leg (thigh and drumstick)
2 celery stalks, chopped
1 medium-size onion, diced
8 cups water or 4 cups water and 4 cups
  chicken broth
2 cups cooked brown or white rice
2 cups frozen green peas, thawed
2 garlic cloves, minced
1 tablespoon chopped fresh parsley
1 teaspoon dried leaf thyme
Salt and freshly ground pepper

Combine turkey, celery, onion, and water in a large pan. Bring to a boil and skim off froth. Reduce heat, cover, and simmer 2 hours or until turkey is very tender.

Remove pan from heat. Remove turkey to a plate and let cool slightly. Discard skin and bones. Chop meat into bite-size pieces.

Add meat, rice, peas, garlic, parsley, thyme, salt, and pepper to stock. Bring soup to a boil; reduce heat and simmer 5 minutes.

Makes 4 to 6 servings.

Variation
The bones from a roasted turkey can be used instead of the turkey leg. Add some of the leftover meat to the soup with the rice.

Note
To remove the fat from the soup, cook the turkey the day before and refrigerate stock and turkey separately. The fat will lift off.

OXTAIL SOUP

3 tablespoons bacon drippings
2 oxtails, cut into slices
1 large onion, thinly sliced
2 carrots, cut into 1-inch pieces
2 quarts cold water or stock
2 celery stalks, cut crosswise into halves
1 bay leaf
1 parsley sprig
1 tablespoon all-purpose flour mixed
    with 2 tablespoons cold water
1/4 cup red wine
1/4 teaspoon red (cayenne) pepper or to
    taste
Salt and freshly ground black pepper

Heat bacon drippings in a large soup pot over medium-high heat. Add oxtails, onion, and carrots and cook until browned, stirring occasionally.

Add the water, celery, bay leaf, and parsley. Bring to a boil. Reduce heat, cover, and simmer about 2 hours or until meat is tender.

Remove oxtails, celery, and bay leaf. Discard celery and bay leaf. Remove meat from bones and return meat to soup. Bring to a boil and stir in flour mixture, wine, cayenne, salt, and black pepper. Cook, stirring, a few minutes until slightly thickened.

Makes 4 to 6 servings.

COWBOY COFFEE

1 gallon cold water
5 cups ground coffee

Fill a 1-gallon coffee pot with water and bring to a rolling boil.

Remove pot from heat and add coffee.

Place over low heat until all dry grounds have submerged.

Makes about one gallon.

Note
Myths for settling the coffee grounds: crossing willow sticks on top of pot, adding cold water or egg shells, swinging the coffee pot around in a propeller-type motion, and clenched teeth.

MIGAS

2 tablespoons olive oil
2 tablespoons butter or margarine
6 green onions with tops, chopped
1 jalapeño chile, minced
8 corn tortillas, cut into wedges
8 eggs, lightly beaten
Salt and freshly ground pepper
Avocado, sour cream, and picante sauce
   to serve

In a large skillet, heat oil and butter over medium-high heat. Add onions and chile and cook until softened. Add tortillas and cook until wedges are soft.

Gently stir in eggs, season with salt and pepper, and cook, stirring, until firm. Garnish with sliced avocado, sour cream, and picante sauce.

Makes 4 servings.

Variation
Finely chopped leftover beef roast or steak or crisp-cooked bacon can be added with the eggs.

ONE-EYED BUFFALOES

2 tablespoons butter or margarine,
  softened
8 slices whole-wheat bread
8 eggs
Salt and pepper

Spread the butter or margarine on both sides of the bread.

Place the bread on a cutting board, and using a 3-inch round cookie cutter, remove the center of each of the bread slices.

Heat a griddle and grease lightly. Place the buttered bread on the griddle, including the rounds, and place an egg in the "eye" of each slice. Season with salt and pepper. Cook eggs until area around the yolk turns white; turn and cook until yolk is done.

Makes 4 servings.

BANANA-WALNUT PANCAKES

1 cup buckwheat flour
1 cup all-purpose flour
4 teaspoons baking powder
1 teaspoon salt
1 egg, lightly beaten
1 cup milk
2 bananas, diced
1/2 cup black walnuts or English wal-
    nuts, finely chopped
Maple syrup, additional bananas and
    walnuts to serve

Sift together flours, baking powder, and salt
into a large bowl. Combine egg, milk,
bananas, and walnuts in a small bowl. Add
milk mixture to dry ingredients and stir just
to combine.

Heat a griddle and grease lightly. Drop batter
with a 1/4-cup measure onto hot griddle.
Cook until pancake edges are browned and
top has bubbles. Turn and cook remaining
side. Serve with butter and maple syrup.

Makes 6 to 8 servings.

Note
Black walnuts are a native delicacy from the
walnut tree, which is prized for both its beauti-
ful wood and its nuts. They are available from
local vendors where the tree is found and also by
mail order.

BLUE CORN WAFFLES

1/2 cup blue cornmeal
1-1/2 cups water
About 1-1/4 cups half-and-half
1/4 teaspoon salt
1 cup all-purpose flour
1/4 cup sugar
1 tablespoon baking powder
2 eggs, lightly beaten
Sour cream and strawberry jam to serve

Combine cornmeal and water in a medium-size saucepan. Cook, stirring, over medium heat until thickened, about 20 minutes. Stir in 1 cup of the half-and-half and salt; let cool.

Sift together flour, sugar, and baking powder; stir in eggs, cornmeal mixture, and enough half-and-half to make batter thin enough to pour.

Preheat a waffle iron. Lightly grease hot iron and add batter. Cook according to manufacturer's directions until golden brown. Serve with sour cream and jam.

Makes 8 waffles.

FRENCH TOAST

4 eggs, lightly beaten
1 tablespoon vanilla extract
1 teaspoon ground cinnamon
1/2 cup evaporated milk
8 slices sourdough bread
Syrup or powdered sugar and fruit to
**   serve**

Combine eggs, vanilla, cinnamon, and milk in a medium-size bowl.

Heat a griddle and grease lightly. Dip both sides of bread slices into egg mixture and place on hot griddle.

Cook until lightly browned on bottom and turn; cook again until browned on remaining side. Serve with syrup or powdered sugar and fruit.

Makes 4 servings.

SOURDOUGH PANCAKES

1/2 cup Sourdough Starter (page 84)
2 cups lukewarm water
1-1/2 cups all-purpose flour
2 eggs, lightly beaten
1 tablespoon sugar
1/4 teaspoon salt
1/2 teaspoon baking soda

Combine starter, water, and flour in a medium-size bowl. Cover with plastic wrap. Let stand overnight.

Preheat a nonstick griddle over medium heat. Add eggs, sugar, salt, and baking soda to batter. Mix just to combine. Lightly grease griddle.

Drop batter with a 1/4-cup measure onto griddle. Cook until pancake edges are browned and top has bubbles. Turn and cook remaining side.

Makes about 10 pancakes.

QUICK-DRAW COFFEECAKE

1-1/2 cups all-purpose flour
1/2 cup buckwheat flour
4 teaspoons baking powder
3 tablespoons sugar
1/2 teaspoon salt
1 egg, lightly beaten
1 cup milk
1/4 cup butter, melted
1/4 cup sugar mixed with 1 tablespoon
    ground cinnamon

Preheat oven to 350F (175C). Lightly grease an 8-inch square pan. Sift together flours, baking powder, sugar, and salt into a large bowl.

Add egg and milk and mix to a soft dough. Spoon into prepared pan; spread evenly.

Brush top generously with melted butter and sprinkle with sugar mixture. Bake 25 minutes or until a wooden pick inserted in the center comes out clean. Serve warm.

Makes 4 to 6 servings.

EGGS 'N' THINGS

2 tablespoons butter or margarine
2 tablespoons olive oil
1 cup diced red onion
1 cup chopped green onions with tops
1 cup diced broccoli
1 cup sliced fresh mushrooms
8 eggs, lightly beaten
1/4 cup evaporated milk
1/2 teaspoon dried leaf oregano
1/2 teaspoon dried leaf basil
Salt and freshly ground pepper
1/4 pound Cheddar cheese, shredded
1/4 pound Monterey Jack cheese,
    shredded
Basil or parsley to garnish

Heat butter and olive oil in a large skillet over medium heat. Add red and green onions, broccoli, and mushrooms and cook until softened.

Combine eggs and milk in a large bowl. Add egg mixture, oregano, basil, salt, and pepper to vegetables and cook until set.

Turn off heat, sprinkle top with cheeses, and cover until cheeses have melted. Cut into wedges to serve and garnish with basil or parsley.

Makes 4 to 6 servings.

RYE GRIDDLE CAKES

1-1/2 cups rye flour
1/2 cup whole-wheat flour
4 teaspoons baking powder
1/4 teaspoon salt
2 eggs, lightly beaten
1-1/2 cups milk
Butter and maple syrup to serve

Sift together flours, baking powder, and salt into a medium-size bowl. Beat eggs and milk together in another bowl.

Add dry ingredients to egg mixture. Beat until combined.

Heat a griddle and grease lightly. Drop batter with a 1/4-cup measure onto hot griddle. Cook until pancake edges are browned and top has bubbles. Turn and cook remaining side. Serve with butter and maple syrup.

Makes 6 servings or 18 pancakes.

BUCKWHEAT CREAM CAKES

1 cup buckwheat flour
1 tablespoon sugar
1 teaspoon baking powder
1/2 teaspoon salt
2 egg yolks
1-1/4 cups half-and-half
Maple or boysenberry syrup to serve

Sift together flour, sugar, baking powder, and salt into a medium-size bowl. Beat egg yolks and half-and-half in another bowl.

Add dry ingredients to egg yolk mixture. Beat until combined.

Heat a griddle and grease lightly. Drop batter with a 1/4-cup measure onto hot griddle. Cook until pancake edges are browned and top has bubbles. Turn and cook remaining side. Serve with syrup.

Makes 4 servings or 8 pancakes

MASHED POTATO CAKES

2 cups mashed cooked potatoes
1/2 cup minced green onions with tops
Salt and freshly ground pepper
1 cup all-purpose flour

In a medium-size bowl, combine potatoes and onions; mix well. Season with salt and pepper.

Using your hands, roll the mashed potatoes and onions into balls, and flatten into cakes; coat with flour.

Heat a griddle and grease lightly. Place cakes on griddle and cook until browned on the bottom; turn and brown remaining side.

Makes 4 servings.

BISCUITS 'N' GRAVY

1/2 pound pork sausage
3/4 cup all-purpose flour
2 cups whole milk
Salt and freshly ground pepper
4 Sourdough Biscuits (page 84) or other
  biscuits

In a large skillet, cook sausage over medium-high heat until browned.

Remove the sausages from the skillet and dice. Pour off most of the fat and return diced sausage to the pan. Place over low heat. Stir in flour; cook, stirring, until bubbly. Stir in about 1-1/2 cups milk.

Cook, stirring, until mixture thickens. Add salt, pepper, and enough milk to make a saucelike consistency. Split biscuits and place on four plates. Spoon gravy over biscuits.

Makes 4 servings.

OATMEAL & FRUIT

4-1/4 cups water
1/2 teaspoon salt
1/2 cup raisins
1/2 cup diced dried apples
1/2 cup diced dried apricots
1/4 teaspoon ground cinnamon
2 cups rolled oats
1/4 cup chopped walnuts
Milk and brown sugar or honey

Bring water and salt to a boil in a medium-size saucepan and add fruit and cinnamon. Reduce heat, cover, and cook, stirring occasionally, about 10 minutes or until fruit is tender.

Stir in oats, return to a boil, then reduce heat. Simmer, uncovered, 5 minutes, stirring occasionally.

Stir in nuts. Remove from heat, cover, and let stand 5 minutes. Serve with milk and brown sugar or honey.

Makes 4 servings.

GRILLED LAMB

1 (about 3-lb.) leg of lamb, shank half
1 cup white wine
1/2 cup soy sauce
1/2 cup olive oil
4 garlic cloves, crushed
2 tablespoons grated gingerroot
1 teaspoon dried leaf oregano
1 teaspoon dried leaf basil
1 teaspoon dried mustard

With a sharp boning knife, remove bones from lamb. Be careful to keep meat in as large a piece as possible. Once bone has been removed, slice through and flatten larger pieces in order to make lamb a uniform thickness for grilling.

Place meat in a 13″ x 9″ glass baking dish. Combine wine, soy sauce, olive oil, garlic, gingerroot, oregano, basil, and mustard in a small bowl. Pour mixture over meat, cover, and refrigerate 1 hour.

Preheat grill. Remove meat from marinade and pat meat dry with paper towels. Place meat on grill and cook 10 to 15 minutes. Brush with marinade. Turn meat and cook until the meat is slightly pink when cut in the thickest part or until an instant-read thermometer inserted in thickest part registers 140F (65C) for rare or to desired doneness. Let stand 10 minutes before slicing.

Makes 4 to 6 servings.

GRILLED TRI-TIP ROAST

1 (1-1/2 to 2 lb.) beef tri-tip roast
4 garlic cloves, crushed
1/4 teaspoon salt
1 tablespoon coarsely ground pepper

Preheat grill. Score roast with diamond cuts on both sides. Rub entire roast with crushed garlic, then salt and pepper.

Place roast on hot grill, fat side up, directly over heat to seal in juices. Grill 20 minutes and turn. If roast browns too quickly, move to a cooler area of the grill.

Cook 25 minutes or until an instant-read thermometer inserted in thickest part of roast registers 140F (65C) for rare, or to desired doneness. Let stand 10 minutes, then cut into 1/2-inch-thick slices.

Makes 4 servings.

GARLIC LIVER & ONIONS

2 pounds sliced calf liver
2 eggs
1 cup all-purpose flour
1/2 teaspoon garlic powder
Salt and freshly ground pepper
1 tablespoon olive oil
1/4 cup butter or margarine
2 onions, thinly sliced
4 garlic cloves, crushed

Rinse liver and pat dry with paper towels. Lightly beat eggs in a shallow bowl. Combine flour, garlic powder, salt, and pepper in another shallow bowl. Dip liver in eggs and coat with flour mixture.

In a large skillet, heat olive oil and butter or margarine over medium heat. Add onions and garlic and cook until soft.

Add liver. Cook liver about 3 minutes per side or until browned on outside but still pink when cut.

Makes 4 to 6 servings.

BOILED CORNED BEEF

3 pounds corned beef brisket
1 (12-oz.) can beer
6 carrots, cut into 3-inch pieces
4 bay leaves
1 teaspoon coarsely ground pepper
1/2 teaspoon dried leaf oregano
1/2 teaspoon dried leaf basil
8 small new potatoes
1 head green cabbage, cut into wedges

Add beef to a 4-quart saucepan. Add enough water to cover and bring to a boil. Reduce heat, cover, and simmer 2 hours, adding water as needed.

Add beer, carrots, bay leaves, pepper, oregano, and basil and simmer 1 hour or until meat is tender.

Add potatoes and cabbage and simmer about 15 minutes or until potatoes are soft.

Makes 4 to 6 servings.

MARINATED VENISON ROAST

3 medium-size onions, minced
1 cup chopped green onions with tops
1 cup white wine vinegar
6 cups white wine
5 garlic cloves, crushed
1 teaspoon salt
2 teaspoons coarsely ground pepper
1 tablespoon dried leaf basil
2 bay leaves
1 (2 to 3 lbs.) venison roast

Combine minced and chopped onions, vinegar, wine, garlic, salt, pepper, basil, and bay leaves in a medium-size nonaluminum saucepan. Simmer 3 to 5 minutes. Cool.

Place roast in a large plastic bag. Pour wine mixture over roast. Seal and refrigerate 3 days, turning bag occasionally.

Preheat oven to 325F (165C). Remove roast from marinade and pat dry with paper towels. Discard marinade and place roast in a roasting pan. Roast 2 hours or until a meat thermometer registers 140F (65C) or to desired doneness. Let stand 10 minutes. Cut into slices.

Makes 6 to 8 servings.

STEAK RANCHERO

1/4 cup butter or margarine
1/4 cup olive oil
2 pounds beef flank steak, cut into
    1/2-inch cubes
1 onion, sliced crosswise
4 garlic cloves, minced
2 fresh jalapeño chiles, sliced crosswise
1/2 cup chopped fresh cilantro
3 tomatoes, cut into wedges
1 red or green bell pepper, diced
1 teaspoon ground cumin
Cooked brown rice to serve
Flour tortillas, warmed, to serve

Heat butter and olive oil in a large skillet over medium-high heat. Add steak, onion, garlic, and chiles. Cook, stirring occasionally, about 4 minutes or until steak is lightly browned, but still rare in center.

Add cilantro, tomatoes, bell pepper, and cumin, and cook 2 or 3 minutes or until bell pepper is softened. Serve with brown rice and flour tortillas.

Makes 6 to 8 servings.

Note
For easier slicing, the steak can be partially frozen before cutting into cubes.

JERKY STEW

1/4 pound beef jerky
4 cups water
2 medium-size red potatoes, sliced about
   1/2 inch thick, quartered
4 celery stalks, chopped
1 large onion, thinly sliced
2 garlic cloves, crushed
1/2 cup white wine

On a sturdy surface, pound the jerky with a meat mallet until the jerky separates into shreds.

Bring water to a boil in a large saucepan. Add jerky. Reduce heat, cover, and simmer 1 hour.

Add potatoes, celery, onion, garlic, and wine. Simmer about 1 hour or until vegetables and jerky are tender.

Makes 4 to 6 servings.

Note
Because the jerky is heavily seasoned, no additional salt, pepper, or herbs are necessary.

VENISON STEW

1-1/2 pounds venison steaks
4 cups cold water
1/2 cup distilled white vinegar
2 tablespoons olive oil
4 cups boiling water
4 ounces mushrooms, sliced
2 carrots, sliced
2 medium-size red potatoes, cut into
   2-inch cubes
1/2 cup white wine
4 garlic cloves, minced
1/2 teaspoon dried leaf thyme
1 green bell pepper, chopped
6 green onions with tops, chopped

Cut the venison into 1-1/2-inch cubes. Place venison in a large nonaluminum bowl. Add cold water and vinegar and let stand 2 hours. Drain venison and pat dry with paper towels.

Heat olive oil in a large saucepan over medium-high heat. Add venison in batches and cook until browned, turning.

Add boiling water, mushrooms, carrots, potatoes, wine, garlic, and thyme. Bring to a boil. Reduce heat, cover, and simmer 1 hour. Add bell pepper and onions and cook 15 minutes or until venison is tender.

Makes 4 to 6 servings.

Note
Soaking venison in water and vinegar removes the wild or gamy flavor.

WHISKEY & MUSTARD STEAK

3 tablespoons Dijon mustard
1-1/2 tablespoons whiskey
1 tablespoon minced garlic
1 (1-1/2-lb.) beef sirloin steak
Coarsely ground pepper

Combine mustard, whiskey, and garlic in a small bowl.

Spread mustard mixture on both sides of steak.

Sprinkle liberally with pepper. Let stand at room temperature 30 minutes or cover and refrigerate up to 8 hours. Preheat grill. Grill steak 10 minutes or until browned. Turn and grill remaining side 10 minutes for medium or to desired doneness.

Makes about 4 servings.

BUFFALO CHILE BURGERS

1-1/2 pounds ground buffalo
1/4 cup minced onion
1 garlic clove, minced
1/4 cup ketchup
1 teaspoon Worcestershire sauce
Freshly ground pepper
1 (8-oz.) can whole green chiles, drained,
  sliced
6 slices Monterey Jack cheese

Preheat grill. Combine ground buffalo, onion, garlic, ketchup, Worcestershire sauce, and pepper in a medium-size bowl.

Shape meat mixture into 6 patties. Grill 5 minutes. Turn and grill 10 more minutes for well done or until almost to desired doneness.

Top burgers with green chiles and cheese. Grill until cheese melts.

Makes 6 burgers.

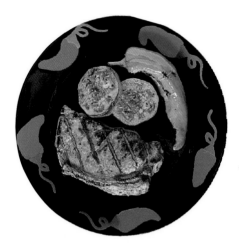

BUFFALO STEAKS

1 cup white wine
1/2 cup olive oil
1/4 cup minced onion
2 garlic cloves, minced
1 teaspoon Worcestershire sauce
1 teaspoon dried leaf thyme
1 teaspoon coarsely ground pepper
4 buffalo loin steaks
2 large tomatoes

Combine wine, olive oil, onion, garlic, Worcestershire sauce, thyme, and pepper in a medium-size bowl.

Place steaks in a large plastic bag. Pour wine mixture over steaks. Seal and refrigerate overnight, turning steaks occasionally.

Preheat grill. Remove steaks from marinade and pat dry. Place steaks on grill. Cook about 10 minutes. Turn and cook 10 minutes for medium or to desired doneness. Cut tomatoes in half and brush with marinade. Grill with steak for the last 10 minutes of cooking.

Makes 4 servings.

Note
Buffalo meat is lean and benefits from a marinade containing oil. Buffaloes are raised on ranches, and the meat is available in some meat markets and by special order.

CHICKEN-FRIED STEAK

2 pounds beef round steak, cut into serving pieces
1/2 cup all-purpose flour
Salt and freshly ground pepper
1/2 teaspoon garlic powder
1/2 teaspoon dried leaf thyme
2-1/2 cups milk
1/4 cup vegetable oil

Pound round steak with a meat mallet to tenderize. Combine flour, salt, pepper, garlic powder, and thyme in a shallow bowl. Pour 1/2 cup milk into another bowl. Heat oil in a large skillet over medium-high heat.

Dip steak into milk, then coat with flour mixture, shaking off excess flour. Add steak to hot oil and cook about 5 minutes or until browned, turn and brown on remaining side. Remove steak and keep warm.

Stir 2 tablespoons of the seasoned flour mixture into skillet. Cook, stirring, until bubbly. Stir in remaining milk and cook until thickened, stirring constantly. Season with salt and pepper. Serve gravy with steak.

Makes 4 to 6 servings.

BEEF STEW & DUMPLINGS

1 pound lean ground beef
1 medium-size onion, finely chopped
3 carrots, diced
4 ounces mushrooms, quartered
1 cup fresh or frozen green peas
1 teaspoon dried leaf thyme
2 cups dry white wine
Salt and freshly ground pepper

Dumplings:
1-1/4 cups all-purpose flour
1/4 teaspoon salt
2-1/2 teaspoons baking powder
3 tablespoons vegetable shortening
About 3/4 cup milk

Preheat oven to 375F (190C). Grease a 3-quart shallow casserole dish. Cook beef, onion, and carrots in a large skillet until beef is browned, stirring to break up meat. Add mushrooms, peas, thyme, and wine. Bring to a boil, reduce heat, and simmer while making dumplings. Season with salt and pepper.

Prepare dumplings: Sift together flour, salt, and baking powder into a medium-size bowl. Cut in shortening until mixture resembles coarse crumbs. Stir in enough milk to make a soft dough.

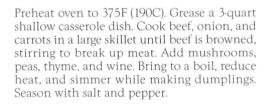

Pour hot stew into casserole dish. Drop dumplings by spoonfuls onto surface of hot stew. Bake about 25 minutes or until dumplings are browned.

Makes 6 to 8 servings.

DUTCH-OVEN MEATLOAF

2 pounds lean ground beef
3/4 cup milk
1 medium-size onion, minced
1/2 cup bread crumbs
4 garlic cloves, minced
1 egg, lightly beaten
2 tablespoons olive oil
1 teaspoon salt
1/2 teaspoon dried leaf oregano
1 cup ketchup
1 tablespoon brown sugar
1 tablespoon Worcestershire sauce

In a large bowl, combine beef, milk, onion, bread crumbs, garlic, egg, olive oil, salt, and oregano. Mix well.

Preheat a 12-inch Dutch oven, including lid (page 8), grease lightly, and pat the beef mixture into bottom of oven. Cover with lid and add hot charcoal briquettes to top (page 9). Set Dutch oven over hot charcoal briquettes (page 9) and bake 1 hour.

In a small saucepan, combine ketchup, brown sugar, and Worcestershire sauce and bring to a boil. Pour ketchup mixture over meatloaf. Cover, add hot charcoal briquettes to top, and bake 15 more minutes or until an instant-read thermometer registers 165 to 170F (70 to 75C).

Makes 4 to 6 servings.

Variation
Bake meatloaf in a large Dutch oven or covered roasting pan in a 375F (190C) oven about 1-1/4 hours total cooking time.

DUTCH-OVEN PORK ROAST

2 tablespoons olive oil
1 (1-1/2 to 2 lbs.) pork loin roast, scored
2 medium-size red apples, sliced
1 onion, sliced
5 garlic cloves, crushed
1 (12-oz.) can sauerkraut, drained
1 cup red or white wine

Preheat a 12-inch Dutch oven, including lid (page 8). Place olive oil and roast in Dutch oven.

Cover roast with apples, then onion slices and garlic, and finally with sauerkraut. Pour wine around roast. Cover with lid and add charcoal to top (page 9).

Place Dutch oven over charcoal briquettes (page 9). Cover with lid, add hot charcoal briquettes to top, and bake 1 hour. Add more hot charcoal briquettes to lid and under Dutch oven and bake 30 minutes more or until an instant-read thermometer inserted in thickest part registers 170F (70C). Remove roast to a platter. Spoon sauerkraut mixture into a bowl. Let stand 10 minutes. Slice roast and serve with sauerkraut and apples.

Makes 4 to 6 servings.

Variation
Bake in a large Dutch oven or covered roasting pan in a 350F (175C) oven about 1-1/2 hours.

DUTCH-OVEN RIBS

4-1/4 pounds pork ribs, cut into ribs
1 medium-size onion, quartered
3 carrots, coarsely chopped
3 bay leaves
1 quart water
1 (12-oz.) can beer

Barbecue Sauce:
1 large onion, finely chopped
3 garlic cloves, minced
3 cups ketchup
1/2 cup packed brown sugar
1/2 cup white wine vinegar
1 cup beer
Hot pepper sauce to taste

Preheat a 12-inch Dutch oven, including lid (page 8). Add ribs, onion, carrots, bay leaves, water, and beer. Place Dutch oven over hot charcoal briquettes (page 9). Cover with lid, add hot charcoal briquettes to top (page 9), and bake 1 hour. Add more hot charcoal briquettes to lid and under Dutch oven and cook 30 minutes more or until ribs are fork tender.

Prepare sauce: Combine all ingredients in a medium-size bowl.

Drain ribs; pour sauce over ribs. Cover with lid and cook 1/2 hour or until ribs are very tender and sauce is thickened slightly.

Makes 4 to 6 servings.

Variation
Bake ribs in a large Dutch oven or covered roasting pan in a 375F (190C) oven about 1-1/2 hours total cooking time.

TENDERFOOT BEEF STEW

1/4 cup olive oil
1-1/2 pounds beef cubes for stew
1 medium-size onion, coarsely chopped
3 carrots, cut into 1-inch pieces
1/2 pound mushrooms, halved if large
6 large red potatoes, cut into eighths
1 large tomato, coarsely chopped
1 bay leaf
1 teaspoon dried leaf thyme
1/2 teaspoon dried rosemary
2 cups dry white or red wine
1/2 cup water

Preheat a 12-inch Dutch oven, including lid
(page 8). Add oil and beef; stir to coat.

Add onion, carrots, mushrooms, potatoes,
tomato, bay leaf, thyme, and rosemary. Stir to
combine.

Add wine and water. Set Dutch oven over hot
charcoal briquettes (page 9). Cover with lid,
add hot charcoal briquettes to top (page 9),
and bake 1 hour. Add more hot charcoal briquettes to top and under Dutch oven and
bake 30 minutes more or until beef is tender.

Makes about 6 servings.

Variation
Bake in a large Dutch oven or covered roasting
pan in a 375F (190C) oven about 1-1/2 hours.

SONORAN RABBIT STEW

2 tablespoons olive oil
1 rabbit, cut into serving pieces
4 cups boiling water
2 potatoes, sliced
1 onion, diced
1 cup fresh or frozen whole-kernel corn
1/2 cup white wine
2 garlic cloves, minced
1 teaspoon crushed red chiles or to taste
1/2 teaspoon ground cumin
1 mild green chile, chopped
Cilantro to garnish

Preheat a Dutch oven, including lid (page 8). Add oil to Dutch oven and add rabbit. Set Dutch oven over hot charcoal briquettes (page 9) and cook rabbit until browned, turning as needed.

Add water, potatoes, onion, corn, wine, garlic, crushed chiles, and cumin. Cover with lid, add hot charcoal briquettes to top (page 9), and bake 1 hour.

Add green chile. Cover, add hot charcoal briquettes to top, and cook 15 minutes more or until rabbit and vegetables are tender. Spoon into bowls and garnish with cilantro.

Makes 4 to 6 servings.

Variation
Bake in a large Dutch oven or covered roasting pan in a 375F (190C) oven about 1-1/4 hours.

QUICK BARBECUED CHICKEN

1 chicken, cut into serving pieces
1 onion, diced
1 cup white wine
4 garlic cloves, minced
4 bay leaves
1 tablespoon chopped fresh parsley
1 tablespoon dried leaf oregano
2 cups ketchup
2 cups barbecue sauce
Steamed white rice to serve

Rinse chicken with cold water and pat dry
with paper towels. Place chicken in a large
pan and cover with water.

Bring water to a boil and add onion, wine,
garlic, bay leaves, parsley, and oregano.
Reduce heat and simmer 45 minutes, or until
chicken is tender when pierced with a fork.

Pour off water leaving about 2 inches in bottom of pan. Add ketchup and barbecue sauce
and return to low heat. Cook 15 minutes, stirring often to prevent sticking. Discard bay
leaves. Serve with rice.

Makes 4 to 6 servings.

BRAISED QUAIL

8 quail, boned
1/4 pound bacon, diced
1 celery stalk, diced
1/2 teaspoon dried leaf thyme
Salt and freshly ground pepper
3 cups water
2 tablespoons butter or margarine,
**   softened**
2 tablespoons all-purpose flour

Rinse quail. Add bacon to a medium-size skillet over medium-high heat. Add quail to skillet with bacon. Cook until bacon and quail are browned, turning to brown all sides.

Place quail in a casserole dish large enough to hold quail without crowding; add celery, thyme, salt, pepper, and water. Cover and cook 1 hour at 300F (150C) or until meat thermometer inserted in thickest part of thigh registers 175F (80C) and quail is tender.

Remove the quail to a serving dish; keep warm. Pour pan juices into a saucepan. Make a paste with butter and flour. Stir into pan juices to make a sauce. Pour sauce over the quail.

Makes 4 servings.

DUTCH-OVEN CHICKEN

1/2 cup butter or margarine
2 tablespoons olive oil
1 chicken, cut into serving pieces
Salt and freshly ground pepper
1/4 teaspoon garlic powder
4 red potatoes, quartered
2 onions, sliced
4 garlic cloves, minced
2 bay leaves
1/4 teaspoon dried leaf oregano
1/4 teaspoon dried leaf basil
1/2 cup white wine

Preheat a 10-inch Dutch oven, including cover (page 8). Add butter and olive oil to Dutch oven. Rinse chicken and pat dry with paper towels. Season chicken with salt, pepper, and garlic powder and add chicken to oil mixture.

Arrange potatoes and onions around chicken and add garlic, bay leaves, oregano, and basil. Pour wine into Dutch oven.

Set Dutch oven over hot charcoal briquettes (page 9). Cover with lid, add hot charcoal briquettes to top (page 9), and bake 1 hour. Add more hot charcoal briquettes to lid and under Dutch oven and cook 30 minutes more or until an instant-read thermometer inserted in thickest part of thigh (not touching bone) registers 175F (80C).

Makes 4 to 6 servings.

Variation
Bake, covered, in a large Dutch oven in a 375F (190C) oven about 1-1/2 hours.

BAKED JUNIPER CHICKEN

4 chicken breast halves
1/4 cup white wine
4 garlic cloves, crushed
1 tablespoon coarsely ground pepper
2 juniper berries, finely ground
1/2 lemon, thinly sliced

Preheat oven to 375F (190C). Rinse chicken and pat dry with paper towels. Place chicken skin side up in a shallow baking dish. Add wine and cover chicken with garlic, pepper, and ground juniper berries.

Place lemon slices on chicken and bake 30 minutes. Remove lemon slices and set aside. Turn chicken and replace lemon slices; cook chicken 20 minutes more or until browned and juices run clear when chicken is pierced.

Makes 4 servings

LEMON-JALAPEÑO CHICKEN

1/2 cup fresh lemon juice
5 garlic cloves, crushed
3 fresh jalapeño chiles, minced
1 chicken, cut into serving pieces
1/4 teaspoon salt
1/2 teaspoon freshly ground pepper

Preheat grill. Combine lemon juice, garlic, and chiles in a blender and blend until smooth.

Rinse chicken and pat dry. Season chicken pieces with salt and pepper. Place chicken on grill. Brush liberally with chile mixture.

Cook 25 minutes, then turn. Cook another 25 minutes or until meat near thigh bone is no longer pink when cut.

Makes 4 servings.

ROASTED WILD DUCK

1 (about 3-lb.) duck, ready to cook
1/4 cup butter or margarine, softened
1 cup all-purpose flour
1 teaspoon salt
1 teaspoon freshly ground pepper
1/2 cup whole cranberry sauce
Fresh parsley to garnish

Preheat oven to 425F (220C). Rinse duck and pat dry with paper towels. Spread outside of duck with butter. Combine flour, salt, and pepper in a baking pan. Coat duck with seasoned flour.

Place cranberry sauce in cavity of duck. Truss duck.

Place duck in a shallow roasting pan. Roast 25 to 30 minutes or until browned and a meat thermometer inserted in thickest part of thigh (not touching bone) registers 175F (80C). Pour off fat once or twice during cooking. Garnish with parsley.

Makes 4 servings.

CHILE CHICKEN STEW

2 tablespoons olive oil
1 (3-lb.) chicken, cut into serving pieces
1 large onion, chopped
1 garlic clove, minced
6 mild green chiles, roasted, peeled, and
  chopped
1 (29-oz.) can hominy, preferably
  Mexican style, drained
1 (14-oz.) can chopped tomatoes
4 cups chicken broth
2 teaspoons dried leaf oregano
1 teaspoon salt
Freshly ground pepper
Cilantro to garnish
Corn tortillas, warmed, to serve

Heat oil in a large Dutch oven over medium heat. Add chicken in batches; cook until browned, turning. Add onion and garlic. Cook 5 minutes, stirring occasionally.

Add chiles, hominy, tomatoes, broth, oregano, salt, and pepper. Simmer about 1 hour or until chicken and onion are tender. Spoon into bowls. Sprinkle with cilantro and serve with tortillas.

Makes 6 to 8 servings.

DOVES IN WINE SAUCE

3/4 cup olive oil
1/2 cup chopped cilantro
2 jalapeño chiles, chopped
2 garlic cloves, crushed
1 teaspoon crushed hot red chiles or to taste
1/2 teaspoon salt
8 dove breasts or 4 squab breasts
1 cup white wine

Combine 1/2 cup of the olive oil, cilantro, jalapeño chiles, garlic, crushed chiles, and salt in a blender. Process until pureed.

Rinse doves and pat dry with paper towels. Place doves in a bowl. Pour puree over doves and turn to coat. Let stand at room temperature up to 30 minutes.

Heat remaining olive oil in a large skillet over medium heat. Add doves and cook until browned, turning. Add wine, reduce heat, cover, and simmer about 20 minutes or until doves are tender. Arrange 2 dove breasts on each plate and spoon any remaining cooking juices over doves.

Makes 4 servings.

FRIED CATFISH & ONIONS

2 pounds catfish fillets
2 eggs
1 cup cornmeal
Salt and freshly ground pepper
Vegetable oil for frying
2 bunches green onions with tops,
   chopped
4 garlic cloves, minced

Rinse fish and pat dry with paper towels.
Lightly beat eggs in a shallow bowl. Combine
cornmeal, salt, and pepper in another shallow bowl. Dip fish in egg, then coat with
cornmeal mixture.

Add 2 inches of oil to a large skillet. Heat oil
to 365F (185C) or until a 1-inch bread cube
turns golden brown in 50 seconds. Add fish
in batches and cook in oil until golden
brown and fish just begins to flake when
pierced with a fork in thickest part. Drain
fish on paper towels.

Heat 1 tablespoon oil in a small skillet, add
onions and garlic, and cook until softened.
Spoon onions and garlic over fish and serve.

Makes 4 to 6 servings.

BAKED TROUT WITH LEMON

2 tablespoons olive oil
1/2 to 1 cup butter or margarine
6 (10-inch) trout, ready to cook
4 garlic cloves, crushed
1 lemon, sliced
Salt and freshly ground pepper

Preheat a 12-inch Dutch oven, including lid. Add olive oil and butter to preheated Dutch oven (page 8) and stir until butter melts. Add trout in a single layer.

Spread crushed garlic over trout and cover with lemon slices. Season with salt and pepper. Place Dutch oven over hot charcoal briquettes (page 9). Cover with lid and add hot charcoal briquettes to top (page 9).

Bake 1 hour or until fish begins to flake when pierced with a fork in thickest part.

Makes 6 servings.

Variation
Bake trout in a large Dutch oven or covered roasting pan in a 400F (205C) oven about 30 minutes or until trout tests done (see above).

CLIFFORD'S SALMON PATTIES

1 (14-oz.) can pink salmon, drained
1 medium-size onion, diced
1 cup fine cracker crumbs
2 eggs, lightly beaten
2 garlic cloves, crushed
1 tablespoon olive oil
Salt and freshly ground pepper
1/2 cup crushed potato chips

In a large bowl, combine all of the ingredients except the potato chips. Mix well and form into patties 1/2 inch thick.

Roll patties in potato chips and lightly press in crumbs with your hands.

Heat a griddle over medium heat and grease lightly. Place salmon patties on hot griddle; cook until browned on bottom. Turn and cook until lightly browned.

Makes 4 patties.

BAKED SQUASH

1 acorn squash, quartered
1/4 cup butter or margarine, softened
1 teaspoon coarsely ground pepper
**1/2 cup crumbled feta cheese or other
  shredded cheese**

Quarter the squash and remove the seeds and
stringy portions.

Place squash shell side down in a baking pan.
Spread butter and pepper over squash. Cover
and bake about 1 hour or until squash is soft.

Place 2 tablespoons feta cheese in the hollow
of each squash quarter, cover, and let stand 5
minutes or until cheese has melted.

Makes 4 servings.

SPICY FRIED POTATOES

2 tablespoons olive oil
2 tablespoons butter or margarine
3 large red potatoes, sliced
1 medium-size onion, sliced
2 garlic cloves, crushed
1 tablespoon crushed hot red chiles or
   to taste
1 teaspoon dried leaf oregano
1 teaspoon dried leaf basil
2 medium-size tomatoes, cubed

Heat oil and butter in a large skillet over medium-high heat. Add potatoes, onion, and garlic and cook about 10 minutes or until onion is soft.

Add chiles, oregano, and basil. Cover and cook over low heat about 10 minutes until potatoes are almost tender.

Add tomatoes and cook until tomatoes are soft.

Makes 4 servings.

GRILLED CORN

4 large ears of corn, in husks
2 quarts water

Trim the silk from the husks and soak in water for 1 hour prior to grilling.

Preheat grill. Remove corn from water, drain, and place on hot grill. Cook over hot coals 10 minutes and turn. Cook 10 minutes or until the husks appear dry.

Remove from grill, remove husks, and serve.

Makes 4 to 6 servings.

CHEESY POTATOES & ONIONS

2 tablespoons butter or margarine
2 tablespoons olive oil
3 garlic cloves, crushed
4 large red potatoes, sliced
4 large onions, sliced
Salt and freshly ground pepper
1 cup shredded Cheddar cheese

Preheat a 10-inch Dutch oven, including lid (page 8). Combine butter, oil, and garlic in Dutch oven.

Place a layer of sliced potatoes in bottom of Dutch oven, followed by a layer of onions. Add the remaining potatoes and onions in alternating layers. Season with salt and pepper.

Set Dutch oven over hot charcoal briquettes (page 9). Cover with lid, add hot charcoal briquettes to top (page 9), and bake 1 hour. Sprinkle cheese over potatoes and onions. Cover, add hot charcoal briquettes to top (but not under Dutch oven), and bake 30 minutes or until potatoes are tender.

Makes 4 to 6 servings.

Variation
Bake, covered, in a large Dutch oven or casserole dish in a 375F (190C) oven about 1-1/2 hours.

HASH BROWN POTATOES

2 tablespoons vegetable oil
4 cups finely chopped potatoes
1-1/2 tablespoons all-purpose flour
1 teaspoon salt
Cilantro sprigs to garnish

Heat oil in a medium-size skillet over medium heat. Combine potatoes, flour, and salt in a medium-size bowl and press potato mixture firmly into pan.

Cook potatoes about 15 minutes or until golden brown on bottom, and turn. Cook about 10 minutes or until bottom has turned golden brown. Turn out from pan onto a plate. Garnish with cilantro and serve hot.

Makes 4 servings.

Note
A well-seasoned cast-iron or nonstick skillet works the best for this recipe.

GRILLED CHILES

4 large mild green chiles

Preheat grill. Rinse chiles and pat dry with paper towels. Place chiles on hot grill.

Grill chiles about 5 minutes or until blistered. Turn and continue grilling 5 minutes or until the chile skin is blistered evenly.

Remove from heat and cool. Remove skins and leave peeled chiles whole or cut into strips. Serve as a vegetable or use in other dishes.

Makes 4 servings.

Note
If you want to do several chiles at a time, they can be cooled and then packed into plastic freezer bags for freezing. Peel the chiles after thawing.

CREAMY MASHED POTATOES

2 pounds russet potatoes
1/2 cup half-and-half
1/2 cup butter or margarine
1/4 teaspoon salt
1/2 teaspoon freshly ground pepper

Peel and quarter potatoes.

Place potatoes in a large saucepan. Add enough water to cover. Bring to a boil, reduce heat, cover, and simmer 30 minutes or until potatoes are soft. Remove from heat and drain.

Combine potatoes, half-and-half, and butter in a medium-size bowl. Mash until all lumps have been removed. Season with salt and pepper.

Makes 4 to 6 servings.

Variation
Stir in chopped fresh herbs to season potatoes.

WILTED GREENS

1 (10-oz.) package fresh spinach, large
   stems removed
1 bunch watercress, large stems removed
6 bacon slices, diced
1/4 cup cider vinegar
2 tablespoons water
2 green onions with tops, chopped
Salt and freshly ground pepper
1 teaspoon sugar (optional)

Rinse spinach and watercress thoroughly and
pat dry with paper towels.

In a small skillet, fry bacon over medium
heat until crisp. Add vinegar and water and
heat until hot.

Combine spinach, watercress, onions, salt,
pepper, and sugar, if using, in a bowl. Pour
hot mixture over greens; toss until wilted.

Makes 4 to 6 servings.

RUBY'S COTTAGE COLE SLAW

3 cups shredded cabbage
1 cup well-drained cottage cheese
1/2 cup shredded carrot
1/4 cup diced green bell pepper
1 teaspoon minced onion
1/2 cup mayonnaise
1 tablespoon cider vinegar
1 teaspoon sugar
Salt and freshly ground pepper
About 1/4 cup half-and-half
6 lettuce leaf cups (optional)

Combine cabbage, cottage cheese, carrot, bell pepper, and onion in a medium-size bowl.

Combine mayonnaise, vinegar, sugar, salt, and pepper in a small bowl. Add enough half-and-half to thin to the desired consistency.

Pour dressing over cabbage mixture. Toss together until coated with dressing and serve in lettuce cups, if using.

Makes 4 to 6 servings.

WHITE CORN SALAD

3 ears white corn
1 cup shredded zucchini
1 (8-oz.) can sliced ripe olives, drained
4 plum tomatoes, diced
1/2 red onion, thinly sliced
1/2 cup red wine vinegar
1/4 cup olive oil
2 garlic cloves, crushed
1/2 teaspoon coarsely ground pepper
1/4 teaspoon salt
1/4 teaspoon sugar
4 avocados

In a large saucepan, cook corn in boiling water 3 minutes. Cut off kernels. Combine corn, zucchini, olives, tomatoes, and onion in a medium-size bowl.

In a small bowl, whisk together vinegar, olive oil, garlic, pepper, salt, and sugar. Add to corn mixture and toss gently. Cover and refrigerate until chilled.

Cut avocados in half, remove pits, and peel. Spoon salad into avocado halves.

Makes 8 servings.

CALAMITY JAN'S RICE SALAD

1/2 cup wild rice
2 cups water
1/2 teaspoon salt
2 medium-size tomatoes, diced
1 large jalapeño chile, chopped
1 bunch green onions with tops,
    chopped
1/2 cup (2 oz.) shredded Monterey Jack
    cheese
1/2 cup (2 oz.) shredded sharp Cheddar
    cheese
1/3 cup cilantro, minced
Cilantro sprigs to garnish

Place rice, water, and salt in a heavy medium-size saucepan and bring to a boil. Reduce heat, cover, and simmer 45 minutes. Drain rice and return to heat to dry, stirring with a fork. Set aside.

Combine rice, tomatoes, chile, onions, cheeses, and minced cilantro in a salad bowl. Cover and refrigerate until chilled. Garnish with cilantro sprigs before serving.

Makes 4 servings.

RED BEANS & RICE

2 cups dried red beans
6 cups water
1 medium-size onion, diced
2 to 4 slices bacon, diced
4 serrano chiles, sliced
4 garlic cloves, sliced
1/2 teaspoon salt
1/2 teaspoon coarsely ground pepper
1/2 cup chopped fresh cilantro
Steamed white rice to serve

Sort beans and remove any rocks or discolored beans. Rinse beans. Place beans in a large pan, add enough water to cover, and soak overnight. Drain beans.

In a large saucepan, boil beans and 6 cups water 10 minutes. Reduce heat, cover, and simmer 1 hour.

Add onion, bacon, chiles, garlic, salt, and pepper and simmer 45 minutes. Add cilantro and cook 15 minutes or until beans are tender. Serve on a bed of rice.

Makes 4 to 6 servings.

BAKED BEANS

2-1/2 cups dried Great Northern beans,
   soaked overnight and drained
1 large onion, chopped
1 (8-oz.) can tomato sauce
2 tablespoons white wine vinegar
3 tablespoons brown sugar
1 teaspoon salt
1 garlic clove, minced
1 bacon slice (optional), finely chopped
1 bay leaf
1 teaspoon peppercorns
3 whole cloves

Place beans in a large pan with enough water
to cover. Boil 10 minutes. Reduce heat, cover,
and simmer about 1-1/2 hours or until beans
are tender, adding more water as needed.
Drain beans, reserving liquid.

Preheat oven to 375F (190C). Combine beans,
onion, tomato sauce, vinegar, sugar, salt, garlic, and bacon, if using, in a 2-1/2-quart casserole dish. Add enough bean cooking liquid
to cover beans.

Tie bay leaf, peppercorns, and cloves in a
cheesecloth bag. Add to beans. Cover and
bake about 1 hour or until beans are very
tender and sauce has thickened. Remove
cheesecloth bag.

Makes about 6 servings.

COWBOY BEANS

2 cups dried pinto beans, soaked
  overnight and drained
1 ham hock
1 tablespoon vegetable oil
1 large onion, chopped
1 garlic clove, minced
1 (14-oz.) can chopped tomatoes
1 teaspoon salt
1 teaspoon ground cumin
1 teaspoon ground dried mild chiles

Place beans and ham hock in a large pan
with enough water to cover. Bring to a boil;
boil 10 minutes. Reduce heat, cover, and simmer about 1-1/2 hours or until beans are
almost tender. Remove ham hock; cool. Cut
meat from bone, discarding skin and bone.
Add meat to beans.

Heat oil in a medium-size skillet over low
heat. Add onion and garlic; cook, stirring
occasionally, until softened.

Add onion mixture to beans with remaining
ingredients. Cook over low heat, stirring
occasionally, about 45 minutes. Beans should
be very soft.

Makes about 6 servings.

RANCHER'S CORN

4 to 6 ears fresh corn
2 bacon slices, diced
1/2 green bell pepper, diced
1/2 red bell pepper, diced
4 green onions with tops, finely
  chopped

Cut kernels from cobs and scrape cobs.

In a large skillet, cook bacon over medium heat until partially cooked. Add bell peppers and onions and cook, stirring occasionally, about 5 minutes or until vegetables are softened and bacon is crisp.

Add corn to skillet and stir to combine. Cover and cook over low heat about 20 minutes or until corn is tender, stirring occasionally.

Makes 4 to 6 servings.

FRIED APPLES

**2 tablespoons butter or margarine
6 red cooking apples such as Winesap or
  McIntosh, sliced
1/2 cup sugar or to taste
1/4 cup white wine
1 teaspoon grated lemon peel**

Melt butter in a large skillet over medium heat. Add apples and cook, covered, about 10 minutes or until apples are softened, stirring occasionally.

Stir in sugar, wine, and lemon peel. Cook, uncovered, about 5 minutes or until liquid evaporates and apples are tender, stirring occasionally. Serve apples warm or at room temperature.

Makes 4 to 6 servings.

DANDELION GREENS

**2 bunches dandelion greens, about 1
  pound total
4 bacon slices, diced
1/2 cup chopped onion
1 garlic clove, minced
1 large tomato, diced
Salt and freshly ground pepper**

Rinse greens thoroughly, pat dry, and coarsely chop.

Combine bacon, onion, and garlic in a large saucepan. Cook over medium heat until bacon is crisp. Drain off most of the fat. Add greens and 1/2 cup water. Bring to a boil, reduce heat, cover, and simmer about 15 minutes or until greens are crisp-tender. Stir occasionally and add more water if needed.

Stir in tomato and season with salt and pepper. Cook 2 minutes just to soften tomato. Drain off any remaining water before serving.

Makes 4 servings.

CORNBREAD

2 eggs, beaten
2 cups milk
2 cups cornmeal
3/4 cup all-purpose flour
4 teaspoons baking powder
3 tablespoons sugar
1/2 teaspoon salt

Preheat oven to 350F (175C). Butter 2 (8-inch)
square baking pans or 1 (13" x 9") baking
pan. Combine eggs and milk in a large bowl.
Combine cornmeal, flour, baking powder,
sugar, and salt in a small bowl.

Pour flour mixture into egg mixture and stir
just until dry ingredients are moistened.

Pour batter into greased pans. Bake about 30
minutes for 8-inch pans or about 40 minutes
for 13" x 9" pan or until top springs back
when lightly pressed.

Makes 4 to 6 servings.

DUTCH-OVEN BISCUITS

3 cups all-purpose flour
2 tablespoons baking powder
1 tablespoon sugar
1 teaspoon salt
3 tablespoons vegetable shortening
About 1-1/4 cups milk

Preheat a Dutch oven, including lid (page 8). Sift together the flour, baking powder, sugar, and salt into a large bowl; cut in the shortening until mixture resembles coarse crumbs.

Stir in enough milk to make a very soft dough. Turn out dough onto a lightly floured board, knead lightly, and roll or pat out to a thickness of about 1/2 inch. Cut into rounds with a biscuit cutter.

Lightly grease Dutch oven and arrange biscuits in Dutch oven, not touching each other. Set Dutch oven over hot charcoal briquettes (page 9), cover with lid, and add hot charcoal briquettes to top (page 9) and bake about 15 minutes or until biscuits are browned.

Makes 6 servings.

Variation
Bake biscuits in a 400F (205C) oven on a baking sheet 10 to 15 minutes or until browned.

WHOLE-WHEAT BISCUITS

2 cups whole-wheat flour
4 teaspoons baking powder
1/2 teaspoon salt
2 tablespoons vegetable shortening
1 egg, beaten
About 1 cup milk

Preheat oven to 400F (205C). Butter a baking sheet. Combine flour, baking powder, and salt in a large bowl. Cut in the shortening until mixture resembles coarse crumbs.

Stir in egg and enough milk to make a soft dough. Turn out dough onto a lightly floured board, knead lightly, and roll or pat out to a thickness of about 1/2 inch.

Cut into rounds with a biscuit cutter. Arrange biscuits, not touching each other, on baking sheet. Bake 10 to 15 minutes or until browned.

Makes 4 to 6 servings.

SOURDOUGH BISCUITS

1-1/2 cups all-purpose flour
1-1/2 teaspoons baking powder
1/2 teaspoon salt
1/4 teaspoon baking soda
1/4 cup vegetable shortening
About 1/2 cup milk
1 cup Sourdough Starter

Sourdough Starter:
1 (1/4-oz.) package active dry yeast
1 tablespoon sugar
1-1/4 cups lukewarm water (110F, 45C)
1-1/4 cups all-purpose flour

Prepare starter: Dissolve yeast and sugar in water in a large nonmetal bowl (mixture will expand as it stands).

Stir in flour with a wooden spoon to make a batter.

Cover loosely with plastic wrap and let stand overnight (mixture should be bubbly and smell yeasty). Remove 1 cup for biscuits.

Sift flour, baking powder, salt, and baking soda into a medium-size bowl or food processor bowl. Cut in shortening until mixture resembles coarse crumbs.

Add the 1 cup starter and enough milk to make a soft dough. Turn out dough onto a lightly floured board and knead until smooth.

Roll out dough to a thickness of about 1/2 inch. Cut into rounds using a 2-inch biscuit cutter. Lightly grease a baking pan. Place biscuits in baking pan, cover, and let rise until doubled in size, about 1 hour. Preheat oven to 400F (205C). Bake about 15 minutes or until golden brown.

Makes about 15 biscuits.

Note
To keep starter going: Remove 1 cup of mixture for biscuits. Add 1 cup lukewarm water and 1 cup all-purpose flour. Cover and let stand overnight. Pour mixture into a glass container, cover loosely, and refrigerate. If not used regularly, remove 1 cup and replenish with flour and water.

POTATO BISCUITS

**1 large russet potato, peeled
1-1/2 cups all-purpose flour
4 teaspoons baking powder
1/2 teaspoon salt
1/4 cup vegetable shortening
1 egg, beaten
About 1 cup milk**

Preheat oven to 400F (205C). Butter a baking sheet. Cook potato in a small saucepan in boiling water until soft; mash until all lumps have been removed.

Sift together flour, baking powder, and salt; cut in shortening until mixture resembles coarse crumbs. Add potato, egg, and enough milk to make a soft dough. Turn out dough onto a lightly floured board, knead lightly, and roll or pat out to a thickness of about 1/2 inch. Cut into rounds with a biscuit cutter.

Arrange biscuits, not touching each other, on prepared baking sheet. Bake 10 to 15 minutes or until browned.

Makes 4 to 6 servings.

SWEET POTATO BISCUITS

1-1/2 cups all-purpose flour
1 cup whole-wheat flour
2 teaspoons baking powder
1/4 teaspoon salt
1/4 teaspoon baking soda
1/4 cup butter or margarine
1 cup mashed cooked sweet potatoes
About 1/2 cup buttermilk

Preheat oven to 400F (205C). Grease a baking sheet. Sift flours, baking powder, salt, and baking soda into a medium-size bowl or food processor bowl. Cut in butter until mixture resembles coarse crumbs.

Add sweet potatoes and enough buttermilk to make a soft dough. Turn out dough onto a lightly floured board and knead until smooth.

Roll out dough into a 12″ x 9″ rectangle. Cut into 3-inch squares. Place biscuits on baking sheet. Bake about 15 minutes or until golden brown.

Makes 12 biscuits.

Note
The amount of buttermilk will depend on how moist the mashed sweet potatoes are. Either freshly cooked or canned unsweetened sweet potatoes can be used.

SOURDOUGH BREADSTICKS

1 (1/4-oz.) package active dry yeast
1 tablespoon sugar
1-1/2 cups lukewarm water (110F, 45C)
1 cup Sourdough Starter (page 84)
1-1/2 teaspoons salt
4 to 5 cups all-purpose flour

Dissolve yeast and sugar in lukewarm water in a large bowl. Let stand 5 to 10 minutes or until foamy. Add starter, salt, and 2 cups of the flour and beat until smooth.

Stir in enough flour to make a moderately stiff dough. Turn out dough onto a lightly floured surface; knead about 10 minutes or until smooth and elastic. Grease a large bowl. Place dough in bowl; turn to coat dough. Cover bowl with plastic wrap. Let rise in a warm place about 1 hour or until doubled in bulk. Punch down dough.

Grease 2 baking sheets. Divide dough in half. Roll out each half into a 10″ x 8″ rectangle. Place a rectangle on each baking sheet. Using a long knife, cut each piece crosswise into 1/2-inch wide strips. Cover with plastic wrap. Let rise until doubled in size, about 45 minutes. Preheat oven to 400F (205C). Bake about 20 minutes or until golden brown. Tear or cut apart to serve.

Makes about 40 breadsticks.

Variation
Brush with water or beaten egg and sprinkle with sesame seeds, caraway seeds, or poppy seeds before baking.

QUICK NUT BREAD

1/2 cup butter or margarine, softened
1/2 cup sugar
2 eggs, lightly beaten
2 cups all-purpose flour
2 teaspoons baking powder
1/2 teaspoon salt
1 cup milk
1 cup chopped pecans or walnuts

Preheat oven to 325F (165C). Grease a 9" x 5" loaf pan. Cream butter and sugar in a medium-size bowl until light and fluffy. Add eggs; beat until thickened.

Sift flour, baking powder, and salt into a medium-size bowl. Beat in flour mixture alternately with milk, beginning and ending with flour mixture. Stir in nuts.

Spoon batter into prepared pan. Bake until golden brown and bread springs back when lightly touched in center, about 50 minutes. Let cool in pan 5 minutes. Remove from pan and cool on a wire rack.

Makes 1 loaf.

Note
The loaf is even better if wrapped after cooling and kept until the next day before slicing.

FRESH APPLE MUFFINS

2 cups all-purpose flour
1/2 cup sugar
2-1/2 teaspoons baking powder
1 teaspoon ground cinnamon
1/2 teaspoon salt
1-1/4 cups milk
1/4 cup butter or margarine, melted and cooled
1 egg, lightly beaten
1 cup chopped apple (1 large)

Preheat oven to 400F (205C). Line 12 muffin cups with paper liners or grease. Sift flour, sugar, baking powder, cinnamon, and salt into a medium-size bowl.

Combine milk, butter, egg, and apple in a small bowl.

Stir apple mixture into dry ingredients just until combined. Spoon batter into muffin cups, filling about two-thirds full. Bake about 20 minutes or until browned. Cool in pan 5 minutes before removing.

Makes 12 muffins.

Variation
Add 1/2 cup chopped pecans to batter.

SOURDOUGH ORANGE ROLLS

1 (1/4-oz.) package active dry yeast
1/2 cup lukewarm water (110F, 45C)
1 cup Sourdough Starter (page 84)
1 egg, lightly beaten
1 cup granulated sugar
1 cup butter or margarine, softened
About 4 cups all-purpose flour
Grated peel of 1 orange
3/4 cup frozen orange juice concentrate
1/2 cup powdered sugar
1/2 cup half-and-half

Dissolve yeast in lukewarm water in a small bowl. Let stand 5 to 10 minutes or until foamy. Combine starter, egg, 1/2 cup of the sugar, 1/2 cup of the butter, and yeast mixture in a large bowl. Beat until smooth. Stir in enough flour to make a moderately stiff dough. Turn out dough onto a lightly floured surface; knead about 10 minutes or until smooth and elastic.

Grease a large bowl. Place dough in bowl; turn to coat dough. Cover bowl with plastic wrap. Let rise in a warm place about 1 hour or until doubled in bulk. Punch down dough. Roll out dough into an 11" x 14" rectangle. Combine remaining sugar, butter, and the orange peel. Spread over dough, leaving 1/2 inch border around edges. Roll up dough jellyroll style, starting from one long side. Cut dough into 1-inch-wide circles.

Grease 2 (13" x 9") baking pans. Combine orange juice concentrate, powdered sugar, and half-and-half in a small bowl; pour half into each pan. Place circles cut side down over juice mixture in pans. Cover and let rise about 30 minutes or until doubled in size. Preheat oven to 350F (175C). Bake about 30 minutes or until rolls are browned. Turn pans upside down on pieces of foil; let stand 5 minutes. Use a spatula to remove any remaining topping and spread on rolls.

Makes about 18 rolls.

SHEEPHERDER'S BREAD

1 (1/4-oz.) package active dry yeast
2 cups lukewarm water (110F, 45C)
1/3 cup butter or margarine, melted
1/3 cup sugar
1-1/2 teaspoons salt
6 to 7 cups all-purpose flour

Dissolve yeast in 1/2 cup of the water in a large bowl. Let stand 5 to 10 minutes or until foamy. Add remaining water, butter, sugar, and salt. Stir in 3 cups of the flour; beat until smooth. Stir in enough remaining flour to make a moderately stiff dough. Turn out dough onto a lightly floured surface; knead about 10 minutes or until smooth and elastic.

Grease a large bowl. Place dough in bowl; turn to coat dough. Cover bowl with plastic wrap. Let rise in a warm place about 1 hour or until doubled in bulk. Punch down dough.

Line a heavy Dutch oven with foil; grease foil and inside lid of the Dutch oven. Shape dough into a round loaf and place in Dutch oven. Cover with the lid. Let rise about 1 hour or until doubled in size. Preheat oven to 375F (190C). Bake, covered, 15 minutes. Remove lid and bake about 35 minutes or until loaf sounds hollow when tapped on bottom.

Makes 1 large loaf.

FRY BREAD

2 cups all-purpose flour
2 teaspoons baking powder
1/4 teaspoon salt
About 3/4 cup milk
Vegetable oil for frying
Powdered sugar, honey, or fruit pre-
serves to serve

Combine flour, baking powder, and salt in a medium-size bowl. Stir in enough milk to make a moderately stiff dough.

Turn out dough onto a lightly floured board. Knead until smooth. Cover and let rest 30 minutes. Divide dough into 8 equal pieces. Roll out each piece into a 7-inch circle. Make a hole in the center of each piece.

Heat 1 inch of oil in a heavy skillet over medium-high heat. Add 1 dough circle. Fry until browned on bottom side, then turn and brown remaining side. Drain on paper towels. Serve hot with sugar.

Makes 8 servings.

DUTCH-OVEN PEACH COBBLER

6 large peaches, peeled and sliced
2/3 cup sugar
2-1/2 tablespoons all-purpose flour
1-1/2 teaspoons ground cinnamon

Graham Cracker Crust:
2 cups graham cracker crumbs
6 tablespoons sugar
6 tablespoons butter or margarine,
    softened

Preheat a 10-inch Dutch oven, including cover (page 8). Prepare crust: Combine crumbs, sugar, and butter in a medium-size bowl. Press crust over bottom and about 1 inch up side of Dutch oven.

Toss peaches with lemon juice. Combine sugar, flour, and cinnamon in a small bowl. Add to peaches; toss to combine.

Spoon peach mixture into crust. Set Dutch oven over 6 hot charcoal briquettes (page 9). Cover and place 7 hot briquettes on cover. Bake about 30 minutes or until peach mixture is bubbly.

Makes 6 servings.

Variation
Bake in a 10-inch round pan or baking dish in a preheated 400F (205C) oven about 30 minutes.

MOLASSES COOKIES

1/2 cup shortening
1/4 cup butter or margarine
1 cup plus 3 tablespoons sugar
1 egg, lightly beaten
1/4 cup molasses
1-1/2 cups all-purpose flour
1/2 cup whole-wheat flour
2 teaspoons baking soda
1/4 teaspoon salt
1-1/2 teaspoons ground ginger
1/2 teaspoon ground cloves

Grease 2 baking sheets. Beat shortening, butter, and 1 cup of the sugar until light and fluffy. Beat in egg and molasses.

Sift flours, baking soda, salt, ginger, and cloves over molasses mixture. Mix into a moderately stiff dough. Shape dough into a ball, cover with plastic wrap, and refrigerate 2 hours.

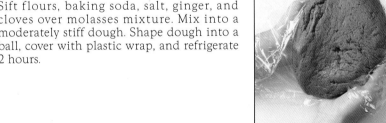

Preheat oven to 375F (190C). Roll dough into balls about 1-1/4 inches in diameter. Roll each ball in remaining sugar. Place about 2 inches apart on baking sheets. Bake about 10 minutes or until browned around edges. Cool on pans 2 minutes, then finish cooling on a wire rack.

Makes about 40 cookies.

RAISIN PIE

2 cups raisins
1-1/2 cups water
1/2 cup sugar
2 tablespoons cornstarch mixed with 2
    tablespoons water
2 tablespoons fresh lemon juice
Grated peel of 1 lemon
1/4 teaspoon salt
Milk

Pastry for double-crust pie:
3 cups all-purpose flour
1 teaspoon salt
1 cup vegetable shortening
6 to 8 tablespoons ice water

Prepare pastry: Combine flour and salt in a medium-size bowl. Cut in shortening until mixture resembles coarse crumbs. Lightly stir in enough water that mixture will form a ball. Wrap in plastic wrap and refrigerate 30 minutes. Preheat oven to 425F (220C). Roll out one-half of dough into an 11-inch circle. Fit dough into a 9-inch pie pan.

Cook raisins and water in a medium-size saucepan over medium heat 5 minutes. Stir in sugar and cornstarch mixture. Cook until thickened and bubbly. Stir in lemon juice, lemon peel, and salt. Pour into pie shell.

Roll out remaining dough into an 11-inch circle. Fit dough over raisin mixture; trim edges. Seal edges and flute. Brush crust with milk. Bake about 30 minutes or until crust is browned and filling is bubbly.

Makes about 8 servings.

Variations
Substitute 1/4 cup chilled butter for 1/4 cup of the shortening.
For a single-crust pie, use one-half the amount of pastry ingredients.

APPLESAUCE CUPCAKES

1/2 cup butter or margarine, room
    temperature
3/4 cup sugar
2 eggs, lightly beaten
1-1/2 cups all-purpose flour
2 teaspoons baking powder
1/4 teaspoon baking soda
1/4 teaspoon salt
1-1/2 teaspoons ground cinnamon
1/2 teaspoon ground cloves
1 cup applesauce
1 cup currants

Preheat oven to 350F (175C). Line muffin
cups with paper liners or grease. Beat butter
and sugar in a large bowl until light. Beat in
eggs.

Sift flour, baking powder, baking soda, salt,
cinnamon, and cloves together. Add to egg
mixture alternately with applesauce, beating
after each addition. Stir in currants.

Spoon batter into muffin cups, filling two-
thirds full. Bake about 20 minutes or until
centers spring back when lightly pressed.
Cool in pan 5 minutes before removing to a
rack to cool completely.

Makes 18 cupcakes.

RANCH-STYLE GINGERBREAD

1/2 cup butter or margarine, softened
1/2 cup packed brown sugar
1/2 cup molasses
2 eggs, lightly beaten
1/4 cup milk
1-1/2 cups all-purpose flour
2 teaspoons baking powder
1/2 teaspoon baking soda
1/4 teaspoon salt
2 teaspoons ground ginger
1/2 teaspoon ground cinnamon
1/2 teaspoon ground allspice

Preheat oven to 350F (175C). Grease an 8-inch square pan. Beat butter, sugar, molasses, and eggs in a large bowl until light. Beat in milk.

Sift flour, baking powder, baking soda, salt, ginger, cinnamon, and allspice over molasses mixture. Beat until smooth.

Pour batter into prepared pan. Bake about 35 minutes or until center springs back when lightly pressed. Center may sink during baking. Cut into squares to serve.

Makes about 8 servings.

Note
Cookie cutters can be used to make interesting shapes.

PEAR STREUSEL PIE

Pastry for single-crust pie (page 96)
1/2 cup sugar
2 tablespoons all-purpose flour
1/4 teaspoon grated nutmeg
1/4 teaspoon salt
4 pears

Almond Streusel Topping:
1 cup all-purpose flour
2/3 cup packed brown sugar
1/2 cup butter or margarine, chilled
1/2 cup sliced almonds

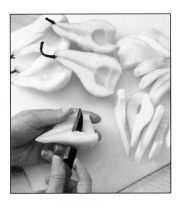

Preheat oven to 375F (190C). Roll out dough into an 11-inch circle. Fit dough into a 9-inch pie pan. Combine sugar, flour, nutmeg, and salt in a medium-size bowl. Peel and core pears; cut into slices.

Add pears to sugar mixture; gently toss to combine. Arrange pears in pastry shell.

Prepare topping: Combine flour and brown sugar in a medium-size bowl. Cut in butter until mixture resembles peas. Stir in almonds. Sprinkle topping over pears. Bake about 30 minutes or until topping is browned.

Makes about 6 servings.

Note
If pears are not used as soon as they are sliced, toss with lemon juice to prevent browning.

BERRY SHORTCAKE

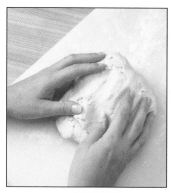

1 quart mixed berries
Sugar to taste
1 pint whipping cream, whipped

Shortcake Dough:
2 cups all-purpose flour
1/4 cup sugar
1 tablespoon baking powder
1/2 teaspoon salt
3 tablespoons vegetable shortening
3 tablespoons butter or margarine,
   chilled
About 1 cup milk

Preheat oven to 450F (225C). Prepare dough: Sift flour, sugar, baking powder, and salt into a medium-size bowl or bowl of a food processor. Cut in shortening and butter until mixture resembles coarse crumbs. Stir in enough milk to make a soft dough. Turn out dough onto a lightly floured surface. Knead lightly about 5 times; do not overknead or shortcake will be tough.

Roll out dough to about a 1/2-inch thickness. Use a 3-inch-round cookie cutter to cut dough into rounds. (Reroll dough as needed.) Place on an ungreased baking sheet about 1 inch apart. Bake 8 to 10 minutes or until puffed and golden brown.

Combine berries and sugar to taste in a medium-size bowl. Split shortcakes. Place bottom halves on dessert plates; top with some berries and whipped cream. Place tops over filling; add more berries and cream.

Makes about 6 servings.

CHOCOLATE OATMEAL CAKE

1 cup regular rolled oats
1-1/2 cups boiling water
1/2 cup butter or margarine
1 cup all-purpose flour
1/3 cup unsweetened cocoa powder
1 teaspoon baking soda
1/2 teaspoon salt
3/4 cup packed brown sugar
3/4 cup granulated sugar
2 eggs
1 teaspoon vanilla extract
Powdered sugar

Combine oats, water, and butter in a medium-size bowl. Cool to room temperature, stirring occasionally. Preheat oven to 350F (175C). Lightly grease a 13″ x 9″ baking pan.

Sift flour, cocoa, baking soda, and salt into a medium-size bowl. Add sugars, eggs, and vanilla to oat mixture. Beat until combined.

Add flour mixture to oat mixture. Beat until combined. Pour batter into greased pan. Bake about 25 minutes or until top springs back when lightly pressed. Cool in pan on a wire rack. Sift powdered sugar over cake. Cut into squares.

Makes about 8 servings.

RASPBERRY JELLYROLL

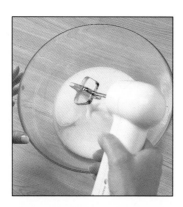

3 eggs
1/2 cup granulated sugar
2/3 cup sifted all-purpose flour
1 teaspoon baking powder
1/4 cup powdered sugar
1 cup seedless raspberry preserves for
    filling
Whipping cream to serve

Preheat oven to 425F (220C). Line a 15″ x 10″ jellyroll pan with waxed paper. Grease paper. Beat eggs and granulated sugar until thickened and lemon-yellow.

Sift flour and baking powder over egg mixture. Fold until combined. Pour batter into prepared pan and smooth top. Bake about 5 minutes or until cake springs back when pressed with fingertips. Sift powdered sugar over cake.

Turn out cake onto a kitchen towel. Remove waxed paper. Roll up cake with the towel, starting at one long side; let cool. Unroll cake and spread with preserves. Roll up, starting at one long side, jellyroll style. Cut in 1-inch slices to serve. Serve with dollops of whipped cream.

Makes about 6 servings.

LITTLE COWPOKE COOKIES

1/4 cup butter or margarine, softened
1/4 cup vegetable shortening
1/2 cup peanut butter
1 cup packed brown sugar
2 eggs, lightly beaten
1 teaspoon vanilla extract
1 cup all-purpose flour
1/2 teaspoon baking soda
1/2 teaspoon baking powder
1-1/2 cups corn flakes
3/4 cup rolled oats
1/2 cup flaked coconut

Preheat oven to 350F (175C). Grease 2 baking sheets. Beat butter, shortening, peanut butter, and sugar until light and fluffy. Beat in eggs and vanilla.

Sift flour, baking soda, and baking powder over egg mixture. Beat until smooth. Stir in corn flakes, oats, and coconut.

Drop cookies by tablespoons onto greased baking sheets about 1 inch apart. Press lightly to flatten. Bake 8 minutes or until firm. Cool on a wire rack.

Makes about 45 cookies.

BUTTERMILK PIE

Pastry for single-crust pie (page 96)
1 cup sugar
2 tablespoons all-purpose flour
2 eggs, lightly beaten
2 tablespoons butter or margarine, room
**   temperature**
1 cup buttermilk
1 teaspoon vanilla extract
Grated nutmeg (optional)

Preheat oven to 375F (190C). Roll out dough into an 11-inch circle. Fit dough into a 9-inch pie pan. Combine sugar and flour in a medium-size bowl. Add eggs, butter, buttermilk, and vanilla. Beat to combine.

Pour egg mixture into pie shell. Sprinkle lightly with nutmeg, if using.

Bake 30 minutes or until a knife inserted off-center comes out clean. Serve warm or at room temperature. Refrigerate any leftovers.

Makes about 6 servings.

WALNUT-MOLASSES TARTS

Pastry for single-crust pie (page 96)
2 eggs, lightly beaten
1/2 cup sugar
1/2 cup molasses
2 tablespoons butter or margarine,
    softened
1/2 cup chopped walnuts

Preheat oven to 375F (190C). Roll out dough into about a 12-inch circle. Cut out rounds using a 3-1/4-inch round cutter.

Press pastry rounds into muffin cups. Combine eggs, sugar, molasses, butter, and walnuts in a medium-size bowl.

Divide filling mixture equally among pastry shells. Bake 20 minutes or until filling is set and crust is browned.

Makes about 8 tarts.

WHISKEY GULCH APPLE PIE

5 or 6 Granny Smith apples (about 2
   lbs.), peeled, cored, and sliced
1 cup sugar
2 tablespoons all-purpose flour
1 teaspoon ground cinnamon
1/2 teaspoon ground allspice
Pastry for a double-crust pie (page 96)
2 tablespoons whiskey
Milk

Preheat oven to 375F (190C). Place apples in a
large bowl. Combine sugar, flour, and spices
in a small bowl. Add to apples and toss to
combine.

Roll out half of dough into an 11-inch circle.
Fit dough into a 9-inch pie pan. Add apples
to pie shell. Drizzle with whiskey.

Roll out remaining dough into an 11-inch circle. Fit dough over apples; trim edges. Seal
edges and flute. Brush crust with milk. Cut
vents for steam to escape. Bake about 50 minutes or until apples are tender and the crust
is golden brown. Serve warm or at room temperature.

Makes 1 (9-inch) pie.

FRIED DRIED PEACH PIES

1 (7-oz.) package dried peaches, chopped
   (about 1-1/2 cups)
2 cups water
1/2 cup sugar
Vegetable oil for frying

Dough:
2 cups all-purpose flour
3/4 teaspoon baking powder
1/2 teaspoon salt
1/2 cup butter or margarine, chilled
About 1/2 cup water

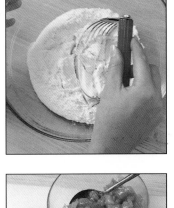

Cook peaches in water in a medium-size saucepan over medium-low heat about 20 minutes or until tender and liquid is gone, stirring occasionally. Stir in sugar. Let cool.

Prepare Dough: Sift flour, baking powder, and salt into a medium-size bowl. Cut in butter until mixture resembles coarse crumbs. Stir in enough water to make a soft dough. Knead dough on a lightly floured board.

Roll out dough to about a 1/4-inch thickness. Cut out 7 (5-inch) circles. Place 2 tablespoons of filling on one-half of each circle. Fold over and seal edges. Preheat 1 inch of oil in a medium-size skillet over medium-high heat. Add pies and fry about 3 minutes or until golden. Turn and brown other side. Drain pies on paper towels.

Makes about 7 pies.

Variation
Place uncooked pies on a baking sheet. Bake in a preheated 425F (220C) oven until golden, about 12 minutes.

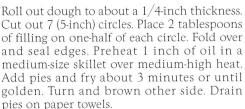
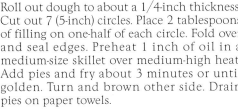

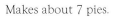

PLUM DUMPLINGS

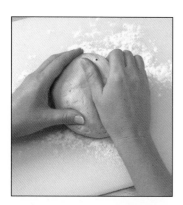

6 prune plums, pitted
6 sugar cubes
Cinnamon

Dumpling Dough:
1-3/4 cups all-purpose flour
1 teaspoon baking powder
1/2 teaspoon salt
1/2 cup butter or margarine, chilled
About 1/3 cup milk

Preheat oven to 375F (190C). Grease an 8- or 9-inch baking dish. Prepare Dough: Sift flour, baking powder, and salt into a medium-size bowl. Cut in butter until mixture resembles coarse crumbs. Stir in enough milk to make a soft dough. Lightly knead dough on a lightly floured board.

Roll out dough to about a 1/4-inch thickness. Cut out 6 (4-inch) squares. Place 1 plum in center of each square. Place a sugar cube in center of each plum. Sprinkle with cinnamon.

Bring opposite corners together and seal edges. Place dumplings in prepared dish. Bake about 15 minutes or until golden.

Makes 6 dumplings.

CHERRY COBBLER

1 cup sugar
2 tablespoons all-purpose flour
2 (16-oz.) cans water-packed sour red
  cherries

Topping:
1 cup all-purpose flour
1 tablespoon sugar
1-1/2 teaspoons baking powder
1/4 teaspoon salt
3 tablespoons butter or margarine
1/2 cup plus 2 tablespoons milk

Preheat oven to 425F (220C). Combine sugar
and flour in a medium-size saucepan. Stir in
juice from cherries. Cook, stirring, over
medium heat until bubbly. Add cherries;
bring to a boil. Pour into a 2-quart shallow
casserole dish.

Prepare Topping: Sift flour, sugar, baking
powder, and salt into a medium-size bowl.
Cut in butter until mixture resembles coarse
crumbs. Stir in enough milk to make a thick
batter.

Drop batter from a spoon onto cherries. Bake
about 25 minutes or until top is browned.

Makes about 6 servings.

BAKED APPLES

4 cooking apples such as McIntosh, Jonathan, or Granny Smith
4 tablespoons light brown sugar
4 tablespoons currants
4 tablespoons finely chopped dried apricots
1/4 cup white wine

Preheat oven to 375F (190C). Core apples and cut a thin strip of peel from center of each apple.

Combine sugar, currants, and apricots in a small bowl. Fill apples with fruit mixture. Reserve any excess mixture and use to fill apples after baking.

Place apples in a small baking dish. Pour wine around apples. Cover and bake about 1 hour or until apples are tender, basting occasionally with pan juices.

Makes 4 servings.

COWBOY'S TEMPTATION

Crushed ice
1 cup apple juice or cider
1/4 cup whiskey
Dash of bitters
Strip of lemon peel
Apple slice (optional)

Fill a tall glass with crushed ice.

Add apple juice, whiskey, and bitters. Stir to combine.

Twist lemon peel to release oil and drop into drink. Garnish with apple slice, if desired.

Makes 1 serving.

Variation
For a hot drink, simmer apple juice, whiskey, and lemon peel together in a small saucepan until hot. Omit bitters and add a cinnamon stick to a mug. Pour in apple juice mixture and serve hot.

METRIC CHARTS

Comparison to Metric Measure

When You Know	Symbol	Multiply By	To Find	Symbol
teaspoons	tsp	5.0	milliliters	ml
tablespoons	tbsp	15.0	milliliters	ml
fluid ounces	fl. oz.	30.0	milliters	ml
cups	c	.24	liters	l
pints	pt.	.047	liters	l
quarts	qt.	.095	liters	l
ounces	oz.	28.0	grams	g
pounds	lb.	0.45	kilograms	kg
Fahrenheit	F	5/9 (after subtracting 32)	Celsius	C

Fahrenheit to Celsius

F	C
200-205	95
220-225	105
245-250	120
275	135
300-305	150
325-330	175
345-350	175
370-375	190
400-405	205
425-430	220
445-450	230
470-475	245
500	260

Liquid Measure to Milliliters

1/4 teaspoon	=	1.25 milliliters
1/2 teaspoon	=	2.5 milliliters
3/4 teaspoon	=	3.75 milliliters
1 teaspoon	=	5.0 milliliters
1 1/4 teaspoon	=	6.25 milliliters
1 1/2 teaspoon	=	7.5 milliliters
1 3/4 teaspoon	=	8.75 milliliters
2 teaspoons	=	10.0 milliters
1 tablespoon	=	15.0 milliliters
2 tablespoons	=	30.0 milliliters

Liquid Measure to Liters

1/4 cup	=	0.06 liters
1/2 cup	=	0.12 liters
3/4 cup	=	0.18 liters
1 cup	=	0.24 liters
1 1/4 cups	=	.3 liters
1 1/2 cups	=	0.36 liters
2 cups	=	0.48 liters
2 1/2 cups	=	0.6 liters
3 cups	=	0.72 liters
3 1/2 cups	=	0.84 liters
4 cups	=	0.96 liters
4 1/2 cups	=	1.08 liters
5 cups	=	1.2 liters
5 1/2 cups	=	1.32 liters

INDEX

Appetizers 11-17

Apple Pie, Whiskey Gulch, 106

Apples, Baked, 110

Apples, Fried, 79

Applesauce Cupcakes, 97

Baked Apples, 110

Baked Beans, 76

Baked Juniper Chicken, 56

Baked Squash, 64

Baked Trout with Lemon, 62

Banana-Walnut Pancakes, 24

Barbecue Sauce, 16

Barbecue Sauce, 50

Barbecued Wings, 16

Beans & Rice, Red, 75

Beans, Baked, 76

Beans, Cowboy, 77

Beef Stew & Dumplings, 47

Berry Shortcake, 100

Biscuits 'n' Gravy, 33

Biscuits, Dutch-Oven, 82

Biscuits, Potato, 86

Biscuits, Sourdough, 84-85

Biscuits, Sweet Potato, 87

Biscuits, Whole-Wheat, 83

Blue Corn Waffles, 25

Boiled Corned Beef, 38

Braised Quail, 54

Bread, Fry, 93

Bread, Quick Nut, 89

Bread, Sheepherder's, 92

Breads 81-93

Breadsticks, Sourdough, 88

Breakfast 21-34

Buckwheat Cream Cakes, 31

Buffalo Chile Burgers, 44

Buffalo Steaks, 45

Burgers, Buffalo Chile, 44

Buttermilk Pie, 104

Cake, Chocolate Oatmeal, 101

Calamity Jan's Rice Salad, 74

Cheesy Potatoes & Onions, 67

Cherry Cobbler, 109

Chicken, Baked Juniper, 56

Chicken, Dutch-Oven, 55

Chicken, Lemon-Jalapeño, 57

Chicken, Quick Barbecued, 53

Chicken-Fried Steak, 46

INDEX

Chicken Stew, Chile, 59

Chile Burgers, Buffalo, 44

Chile Chicken Stew, 59

Chiles, Grilled, 69

Chocolate Oatmeal Cake, 101

Chowder, Corn, 18

Clifford's Salmon Patties, 63

Cobbler, Cherry, 109

Coffee, Cowboy, 21

Coffeecake, Quick-Draw, 28

Cole Slaw, Ruby's Cottage, 72

Cookies, Little Cowpoke, 103

Cookies, Molasses, 95

Cooking in a Dutch Oven, 8

Corn Chowder, 18

Corn Salad, White, 73

Corn, Grilled, 66

Corn, Rancher's, 78

Cornbread, 81

Corned Beef, Boiled, 38

Cowboy Beans, 77

Cowboy Coffee, 21

Cowboy's Temptation, 111

Creamy Mashed Potatoes, 70

Crust, Graham Cracker, 94

Cupcakes, Applesauce, 97

Dandelion Greens, 80

Desserts 94-111

Dough, Shortcake, 100

Doves in Wine Sauce, 60

Duck, Roasted Wild, 58

Dumpling Dough, 108

Dumplings, 47

Dumplings, Plum, 108

Dutch-Oven Biscuits, 82

Dutch-Oven Chicken, 55

Dutch-Oven Meatloaf, 48

Dutch-Oven Peach Cobbler, 94

Dutch-Oven Pork Roast, 49

Dutch-Oven Ribs, 50

Eggs 'n' Things, 29

Fish 61-63

French Toast, 26

Fresh Apple Muffins, 90

Fried Apples, 79

Fried Catfish & Onions, 61

Fried Dried Peach Pies, 107

Fried Mountain Oysters, 14

Fried Rattlesnake, 13

Fry Bread, 93

Garlic Liver & Onions, 37

Gingerbread, Ranch-Style, 98

Graham Cracker Crust, 94

Grilled Chiles, 69

Grilled Corn, 66

Grilled Lamb, 35

Grilled Tri-tip Roast, 36

Hash Brown Potatoes, 68

Hot Hot Salsa, 11

Jellyroll, Raspberry, 102

Jerky Stew, 41

INDEX

Lamb, Grilled, 35
Lemon-Jalapeño Chicken, 57
Little Cowpoke Cookies, 103
Liver & Onions, Garlic, 37

Marinated Venison Roast, 39
Mashed Potato Cakes, 32
Mashed Potatoes, Creamy, 70
Meatloaf, Dutch-Oven, 48
Meats 35-52
Migas, 22
Molasses Cookies, 95
Mountain Oysters, Fried, 14

Nut Bread, Quick, 89

Oatmeal & Fruit, 34
Oatmeal Cake, Chocolate, 101
One-eyed Buffaloes, 23
Onions, Cheesy Potatoes &, 67
Onions, Garlic Liver &, 37
Oxtail Soup, 20

Pancakes, Banana-Walnut, 24
Pancakes, Sourdough, 27
Pastry, 96
Peach Cobbler, Dutch-Oven, 94
Peach Pies, Fried Dried, 107
Pear Streusel Pie, 99

Pie, Buttermilk, 104
Pie, Pear Streusel, 99
Pie, Raisin, 96
Pie, Whiskey Gulch Apple, 106
Pies, Fried Dried Peach, 107
Plum Dumplings, 108
Pork Roast, Dutch-Oven, 49
Potato Biscuits, 86
Potato Cakes, Mashed, 32
Potatoes, Creamy Mashed, 70
Potatoes, Hash Brown, 68
Potatoes, Spicy Fried, 65
Potatoes & Onions, Cheesy, 67
Poultry 53-60

Quail, Braised, 54
Quick Barbecued Chicken, 53
Quick-Draw Coffeecake, 28
Quick Nut Bread, 89

Raisin Pie, 96
Ranch-Style Gingerbread, 98
Rancher's Corn, 78
Raspberry Jellyroll, 102
Rattlesnake, Fried, 13
Red Beans & Rice, 75
Ribs, Dutch-Oven, 50
Rice Salad, Calamity Jan's, 74
Rice, Red Beans &, 75
Roast, Grilled Tri-tip, 36
Roast, Marinated Venison, 39
Roasted Wild Duck, 58
Ruby's Cottage Cole Slaw, 72
Rye Griddle Cakes, 30

INDEX

Salmon Patties, Clifford's, 63

Salsa, Hot Hot, 11

Sheepherder's Bread, 92

Shortcake Dough, 100

Shortcake, Berry, 100

Side Dishes 64-80

Smoked Trout Triangles, 17

Sonoran Rabbit Stew, 52

Soup, Oxtail, 20

Soup, Turkey, 19

Soups 18-20

Sourdough Biscuits, 84-85

Sourdough Breadsticks, 88

Sourdough Orange Rolls, 91

Sourdough Pancakes, 27

Sourdough Starter, 84

Spicy Baked Wings, 15

Spicy Fried Potatoes, 65

Squash, Baked, 64

Steak, Chicken-Fried, 46

Steak Ranchero, 40

Steak, Whiskey & Mustard, 43

Steaks, Buffalo, 45

Stew, Beef, 47

Stew, Chile Chicken, 59

Stew, Jerky, 41

Stew, Sonoran Rabbit, 52

Stew, Tenderfoot Beef, 51

Stew, Venison, 42

Sweet Potato Biscuits, 87

Tarts, Walnut-Molasses, 105

Tenderfoot Beef Stew, 51

Toast, French, 26

Tortilla Appetizer, 12

Trout, Smoked Triangles, 17

Turkey Soup, 19

Venison Roast, Marinated, 39

Venison Stew, 42

Waffles, Blue Corn, 25

Walnut-Molasses Tarts, 105

Whiskey & Mustard Steak, 43

Whiskey Gulch Apple Pie, 106

White Corn Salad, 73

Whole-Wheat Biscuits, 83

Wilted Greens, 71

Wings, Barbecued, 16

Wings, Spicy Baked, 15